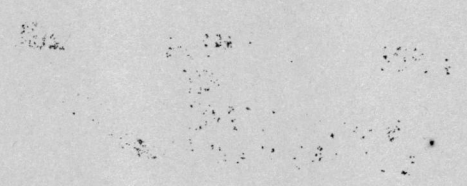

A Woodland Carol

written & illustrated by
Helen Earle Simcox

A Windswept Book
Windswept House Publishers
Mount, Desert, Maine 04660

Copyright 1997 by Helen Earle Simcox
ISBN 1-883650-30-5
Library of Congress Number 96-60478

Printed in the United States of America
for the Publisher by
Downeast Graphics & Printing
Ellsworth, Maine 04605

to my husband

Helen E. Simcox

A Woodland Carol

*Come shining stars
and crown Him King.*

*Come winter birds
and softly sing.*

*Come evergreens
    and round Him ring.*

Jesus, the Savior, is born.

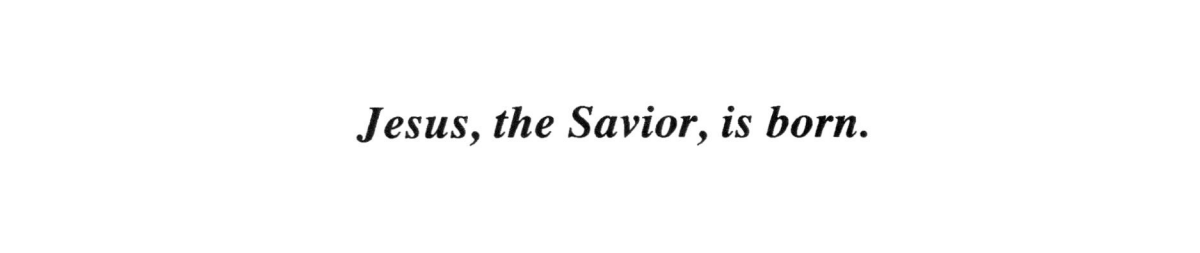

*Fly purple finch
and kinglet, fly.*

    *Come greet the Son
of God Most High
and sing for Him
a lullaby.*

*Fly little owl;
come join the scene.*

    *Follow the starlight's
golden gleam.*

    *Wish for Him
    a sweet, sweet dream.*

*Come red squirrel
and chickadee.*

   *Come to the stable,
come and see
Jesus asleep
on Mary's knee.*

*See little mole
the wondrous sight:
how angels fill
the sky with light.*

    *Come, leave your dark
earth home tonight.*

*Come pretty fox,
forget wild ways.*

*Run to the Master,
give Him praise.*

*Serve Him . . . love Him
all your days.*

*Come little skunk,
you need not hide.*

> *Jesus would like you
> by His side--
> safely . . . closely
> to abide.*

*Come little mice,
be living toys--
playing leap-frog
for Mary's Boy.*

    *Welcome Him
and jump for joy.*

Come cottontail,

raccoon and crow,

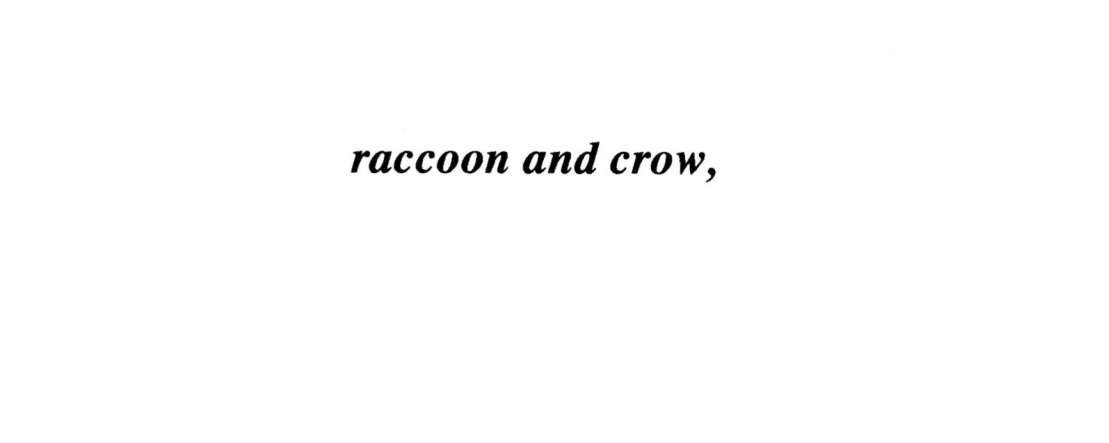

*come porcupine
and white-tail doe.*

*Come every creature--
every thing with
  fur or feathers--
  come and sing.*

Sing
 praises, praises
  to your King.

ABOUT THE AUTHOR

Helen Earle Simcox is the author and illustrator of two picture books: *My Book of Gray* (Windswept, 1989) and *For All The World* (Augsburg Fortress, Minneapolis, 1994). She also edited and illustrated an anthology of black poetry, *Dear Dark Faces* (Lotus Press, Detroit, 1980). She has had poems published in *The Christian Century*, *The Christian Science Monitor* and several literary magazines and anthologies. She resides in Northfield, MN, with her husband, a retired Presbyterian minister.

NORMANDALE COMMUNITY COLLEGE
LIBRARY
9700 FRANCE AVENUE SOUTH
BLOOMINGTON, MN 55431-4399